IT'S NECESSARY
TO NEGOTIATE

I0486231

By

Deborah Siegel

The information provided herein is stated to be truthful and consistent, in that any liability, in terms of inattention or otherwise, by any usage or abuse of any policies, processes, or directions contained within is the solitary and utter responsibility of the recipient reader. Under no circumstances will any legal responsibility or blame be held against the publisher for any reparation, damages, or monetary loss due to the information herein, either directly or indirectly.

Respective authors own all copyrights not held by the publisher.

The information herein is offered for informational purposes solely, and is universal as so. The presentation of the information is without contract or any type of guarantee assurance.

The trademarks that are used are without any consent, and the publication of the trademark is without permission or backing by the trademark owner. All trademarks and brands within this book are for clarifying purposes only and are the owned by the owners themselves, not affiliated with this document.

Table of Contents

INTRODUCTION

Everybody Negotiates Every Day

We were born to negotiate! Since infants we have struggled, persuaded, convinced, and downright fought to get what we want. Some of us were more persistent, more determined to have our own way, but we all developed a unique style of negotiating. As a baby, our negotiations consisted of crying and turning on that big beautiful smile. As a toddler, we branched out a bit and incorporated throwing ourselves down on the floor and kicking our legs until mother caved. Some of us more creative negotiators even resorted to holding our breath until we passed out—very powerful negotiations, and you only had to follow through once for it to become a most effective negotiation tool. The more gentle spirits negotiated with charm, learning to perform, to behave adorably, to be grateful and thankful, and as a result most of their wants and needs were covered.

These early behaviors seemed to set the stage for the style of negotiators we were to become. If your parents and siblings were tough negotiators, you had two ways to go—either dig in your heels until the prize was yours or give up and retreat. It may have also depended on the prize and how badly you desired it. Whatever the case, we were all taught at an early age to negotiate. Some of us became experts at negotiations; some of us—not so much. The beauty of a learned skill like negotiating is that there is always room for improvement.

The better you prepare, observe, and listen before attempting to participate in the negotiations, the bigger your advantage. Good judgement, wise discernment, and that illusive but instinctive inner knowing we call intuition are all important components of successful negotiating. Learning how to come from a point of power, even when you are negotiating with someone who has more authority than you is critical for success, but coming from a point of power doesn't mean bullying the other party or seeing who can shout the loudest. Powerful negotiators know how to use finesse and polish, how to charm, and how to persuade when presenting their point of view or opinion in a difficult negotiations.

If you would like to improve your negotiation skills and yet still be a fair and just partner in the exchange, you've come to the right place. If you want to learn how to handle the fear you feel when negotiating or your need to intimidate in the process of negotiating, keep reading. If you simply wish to overcome your shyness of asking for and expecting more, you're well on your way. Some of you may want to resist the temptation to jump at the first offer, which is usually the sign of low self-esteem or a lack of self-worth. Guess what? We can help with that as well. All you have to do is make a commitment to try a new and better method of negotiating that will allow you to receive your fair share and negotiate with renewed enthusiasm and anticipation.

Chapter One—What Do We Negotiate?

Like I said in the introduction, we negotiate everything. If that's too broad to get your head around, let's cover some of the things you may be negotiating and then take a personal inventory to analyze your success rate. Unless you are an ultra-control freak, you are required to negotiate daily in almost all your relationships. Even the most hard core controllers have to negotiate submissive behaviors from the other party. It's usually done through fear and intimidation, but it's still a give and take negotiations. Whether the exchange is with a spouse, a child, family, friends, or business associates, the negotiations are ongoing.

Negotiating with Your Spouse

This usually is a highly emotional negotiation that can easily go south if you don't set some ground rules. My husband and I have three such ground rules for our negotiations.

1. Each person gets 5-10 minutes to express their point of view or opinion

without the other interrupting or attempting to out shout the other.

2. We agree to practice interactive listening, where we either repeat back major points the other has expressed to indicate we understand and are willing to compromise. Sometimes the interactive listening means we must first clarify understanding before continuing the negotiations. It's surprising how many times we have resolved our issue through fair negotiations by avoiding these types of misunderstandings.

3. We value and respect one another— ALWAYS! Sometimes it might mean one of us giving in to the other's wishes, with a promise to renegotiate at a later date.

Negotiating with a spouse can be most difficult if you use your professional skills to get your way. Professional negotiations are commonly much more rational and require a whole different skillset. Trying to apply logic only to an emotional negotiation creates a "go nowhere" outcome. There's nothing more aggravating than someone calmly sitting back, showing little to no emotional investment when you're at the "all in" point. The calmer one party is, the more the other party's emotions escalate. Learn how to negotiate differently depending on the people, situations, and power positions of those involved.

It surprises me how many relationships survive a take/take attitude, with both parties fighting for the power position in the negotiations. This type of struggle usually ends up in a heated argument instead of a successful negotiation. That's why setting some ground rules is sure to change the outcome and create a more just and fair exchange. One of my associates shared how he and his wife finally began to stop the bickering and devise a plan that put their negotiations on a level playing field. Since his personality was laid back and his wife's was to be more outspoken, he usually gave into the shouting. You would think that she had won the negotiations, but no so. He soon became disenchanted with his marriage, and they began to drift apart. To save their marriage, they turned to a very wise counselor who made the following suggestion. When they were negotiating their wants and needs in the relationship, the moment one began trying to out shout the other, that person forfeited his or her position in the negotiations. You get loud—negotiations over!

Negotiation doesn't have to mean a fight. If you feel like you have to fight with your spouse to get your way, you're not ready for a fair negotiation. Go back to square one and ratchet it down about 20 notches then ask for another time to negotiate. Remember, anger promotes more anger, and it's to nobody's benefit.

Getting your way in one negotiation with a spouse may mean that you must be the compromising party in the next. That's a true give and take, so know your wants and pick your negotiations carefully.

Negotiating with Your Children

This is a whole other ballgame. As a parent, you must realize you are not on even power levels in this negotiation. Although every parent should hold the position of authority, that is not always the case. So, before entering into any more negotiations with your children, ask yourself these five questions:

1. Is my child making a reasonable request, or do I need to play the parent card and insist on doing things my way or the highway?
2. Am I the authority in my child's life?
3. How will my current level of authority impact the negotiations?
4. Are all parties able to respectfully and lovingly practice healthy negotiations at this time?

17

5. Has everybody committed to play by the three ground rules?

Word of warning! If you are not an authority figure in your child's life, you are already at a disadvantage in the negotiations. To avoid being pulled into a negative negotiation, make sure your relationship is on solid ground, and that both you and your child will benefit from the negotiated outcome. There must be a payoff for all parties. If one controls the negotiations, there will be no viable solution and nobody benefits. The issue will raise its ugly head again, and this time your child will be stronger and more determined to fight than negotiate.

Negotiating with Other Family Members

In a negotiation, other family members can be treated similarly to how you close friends—except for an aging mother or father. These types of negotiations usually require a softer approach that is punctuated with empathy and understanding, and here's why. As your parents age, your power positions change and the parent roles can be reversed. In many cases, you become the parent to your aging parents—especially if your parent is ill and you are the caregiver.

The power levels in negotiations such as these are quite complex. It's important that your parent feels empowered, but it is also important that they are protected, which may mean you are in the authority position. Some aging parents refuse to recognize that role reversal and feel the need to fight for the power in a negotiation. That's when you have to know when to push and when to step back and compromise so the parent doesn't feel set aside and useless.

There are also occasions when you should do what I call step up negotiations. You start out with the bottom level negotiations then you take it one step up, then the next step up, until you have reached the level you want without making the other party feel unappreciated or under-valued. This step up method is great to use with aging parents who need to get used to the idea of letting go; doing the step up method allows them to let go a little at a time.

Negotiating with Friends

Negotiating with friends can be tricky if you want to preserve the friendship, especially if you have made the mistake of entering into a business arrangement with them. This happened to me when I opened a business with one of my closest friends. We soon realized that we needed to make other financial arrangements because the business was not supporting both of us. I was the most logical partner to buy her out, so we began negotiating a contract. As usual, we set up ground rules similar to those I gave you previously, except for one. We both agreed that our friendship was more important to us than anything to do with the business and fair treatment was paramount to both of us.

It was a successful buy-out, and we put a special stipulation in the negotiation. Our attorneys thought we were this side of crazy, but it worked well for both of us. Because we had both put our heart and soul into the business for a year and had not drawn a salary, there were few assets to split. I couldn't afford to give her a lot of money at that time for the business, and it really wasn't worth it anyway. So, we negotiated an agreement that gave her a little and cost me a little at the time of our buy-out. I would work the business for the next two years and would take full responsibility for all the debt—also claiming any profits should there be any to claim. If, after two years, she wanted to buy back into the business she had the option to do so at the price she was paid in the buy-out. It was fair for both of us, and we were able to remain the best of friends.

The best thing to do when negotiating with a best friend is to put yourself in their place. Whatever you are offering, would you agree to that if your positions were switched? That one question keeps your negotiations honest and just. Personally, I believe the very best thing is to not mix pleasure and business in the first place; then you never have to worry about losing a lifelong friend over what could well be a temporary business arrangement.

Negotiating Purchases

We have much more experience doing that these days than we did 10 or 20 years ago. With Craigslist, eBay, community yard sales, and outlet malls, holding firm to your price is a thing of the past. I never used to enjoy the whole shopping experience, but now that I can negotiate price, I don't mind browsing the outlets. I believe being able to negotiate price has given me a reason to shop; I simply love the challenge.

Flea markets are another arena where you can practice your negotiating skills. When asked the price of the item, the vendor usually sets the price on the high side. Then the buyer offers a figure that is quite a bit lower. In most cases, it's split down the middle and everybody is satisfied. Notice something? Nobody got exactly what they asked for; everybody compromised but was happy with the negotiations.

That's a successful negotiation—when everyone compromises, gives a little and takes a little, and yet leaves the negotiations feeling good about their transaction. It should always be a feel good. If one party gets everything and the other party walks away with almost nothing, they will be discouraged from ever striking up negotiations with you in the future. Who knows, that may be a much greater loss for you. You may have wonthe battle but lost the war.

This happened to my sister when she was negotiating the price of a chair at the flea market. At the time the vendor seemed desperate to dispose of the furniture, and my sister recognized his need. She offered a ridiculously low price for the chair, and, as expected, the vendor countered my sister's offer. The problem was she was fixed on her priced and refused to negotiate even one dollar off her original offer. The vendor sold her the chair, but he was not happy that she had been so rigid. About three weeks later, she decided she wanted a sofa to go with the chair. She went back to the same flea market in hopes that the same vendor would have a matching sofa. As it turned out he did, and this time he was the one who recognized my sister's need. She needed the sofa that matched that chair. He refused to step off the price even one dollar.

It is my belief, if my sister had negotiated fairly with the vendor to begin with, she probably would have received just as great a discount or even more for her loyalty, and they both would have been happier in the transaction. Each time one party left angry and unwilling to see the other's point of view. Neither of these negotiations was successful or satisfying to both parties. In the future, the vendor may refuse to reduce his price and lose the business, and my sister was so mad she will never do business with that same vendor who actually carried great furniture at a very reasonable price. Everybody lost!

Negotiating Services

This can be confusing, especially when you have not done your homework. Whether you are on the selling end or the buying end, negotiations for services rendered require you to know what the competition is offering. Make sure when doing your homework before the negotiations, that you are comparing apples to apples—same service, same added value. Negotiating services can also be difficult when there is a special talent involved. For example, you may actually like the service of another business but the prices are substantially higher. Let me share with you how my friend once negotiated this situation. She owned an up-scale grooming salon and her prices reflected her hard-earned reputation of having the best groomers in town. Because she used the best products, employed the best groomers, and paid the highest space lease for such a beautiful location, she was forced to pass those costs on to her customers. One potential customer was excited to use her services and absolutely loved the job they did on her dog, but felt she couldn't afford the price. She regularly groomed her dog once a month, and so they negotiated the price down to be more competitive if she agreed to bring the dog every month with a standing appointment. Great negotiations—both parties very happy with the outcome. In fact, my friend actually made much more in the long run. The new customer went on her neighborhood blog and referred everyone to the salon. Everybody benefited!

As an owner, taking a hard line in the negotiations rarely benefits you. It is always better to let customers know you understand their position and are more than willing to work with them to earn their business.

Negotiations for Jobs and Pay Raises

Let's first consider the scenario that you are the candidate, the one looking for the job. The very first thing you must do is know your worth, understand the value that you bring to the negotiating table. If you know your worth and still sell yourself short, then it's on you. Sure, you may get the job, or the pay raise, but you will have an underlying dissatisfaction that could cause you to be looking for another job.

If you are negotiating a job or new position, think about what makes you unique to your industry. What can you do that is unique and could help the company stand head and shoulders above its competition? During the negotiations, be sure to make that difference a focal point. If you can create that additional value with your prospective employer, what he would be paying you is all relative. The extra money he can potentially earn will more than make up the difference. If you don't know your worth, you can't expect your employer to know either.

As a candidate, you walk a fine line between showing your eagerness that could be misconstrued as desperation, and playing it cool so that you are not at a disadvantage in the negotiations for money. I was once offered a job that I knew would be right up my ally. I wanted to accept the position, but the pay was substantially lower than I had in mind. I wasn't shy about telling him how I felt. If I accepted his offer, I feared I would lose enthusiasm for the job because I would feel like I wasn't being paid what I was worth. If I didn't take the job, I felt like I would be missing a great opportunity to work with a creative and innovative team. Because I was honest with my feelings and appealed to him both logically and emotionally, we were able to negotiate a mutually beneficial arrangement. I accepted the job with a promise to review my pay in six months. We set a performance criteria, which promised me a pay raise if I met 90 percent or more of our written objectives during that six-month period. I got to work at a job that I loved with talented people and a wonderful culture, and my employer got an over-achiever whose work ethic was second-to-none and creative spirit was a great addition to his team of professionals. After six months, we didn't have to renegotiate. I let my performance do the negotiating for me. I was automatically bumped to an income that was higher than I would have negotiated in the beginning, making me feel quite appreciated.

Chapter Two—Negotiating
No Nos

Truly understanding what negotiating entails will enable you to avoid nasty negotiating no nos that prohibit forward movement by either party. Negotiating doesn't mean arguing your wants and needs. Negotiating doesn't mean hammering the other party until they cave in and let you have what you want.

Negotiating doesn't really even mean persuading or convincing someone to come to your side. What negotiating is really about is simply this—both parties present their wants or needs and come to an agreement as to what works best for everybody. What works best might be to do nothing at all, and that's okay. The most important thing is that you realize it is about coming to an agreement through compromise. In a successful negotiation, you probably won't get everything you want but neither will the other party to the negotiations. You'll both decide what you are willing to give up in order to get what you want.

So, let's walk through some of the things you never want to do when negotiating. These are definitely negotiating no nos.

1. Resist the temptation to argue your point of view or your opinion. In an argument, nobody wins. If you feel tensions building, do something to change the pace, to give all parties a break. You may want to break for lunch or postpone the negotiations for a few days to give you a chance to do a bit more homework and defuse the anger.

2. Don't enter into a negotiation before you are properly prepared. Know what you want, what you're worth, the words you want to hear from the other party, and what questions you'll need to ask in order to hear those words. Be prepared for the unexpected by role-playing with your spouse or friend until you feel confident and ready.

3. Don't hide something that could negatively impact the possibilities of a successful negotiation. In other words, if you have an issue, get it out on the table along with a suggested solution. Don't wait for the other party to point out what you already know. Do it yourself and show them you have already prepared for that possibility or circumstance.

4. Don't go all in with the first offer in a negotiation. Have the confidence, courage, and credibility to hang in there until you feel like the negotiation is balanced and fair. Fighting past what is fair to either party only causes dissention and dissatisfaction.

5. Avoid beating around the bush; simply and clearly state your wants and

needs so all parties know exactly what is being negotiated. Once those needs and wants are met, don't get greedy and attempt to negotiate more. Most people who get close to what they want and feel as though they are getting what they are worth, need to prove themselves before entering into a counter or renegotiation.

6. Don't be rigid and insistent during a negotiation. It is much more powerful and likely that you will come to a positive outcome when you can be creative in your compromises. Give this thing and ask for that thing. It's like a dance, two steps forward in the negotiations then one step back. If you do that enough, you'll come out on top without making the other party

Deborah Siegel

feel they were cheated or that you took advantage of them.

7. Don't ask for the impossible or unreasonable unless you're prepared to lose everything. Coming across like a know-it-all or a big shot only creates resentment and dislike. You've lost your ability to successfully negotiate before you've even begun. Check your ego at the door.

8. Don't assume the outcome of a negotiation. It isn't over 'til the fat lady sings. If you feel as though you are not gaining ground, get creative. Give the other party a little something in trade for something you want. Negotiating is like riding a rollercoaster—first you're up, then you're down, then you're up again.

Until your car comes to a dead stop, the ride isn't over.

9. Don't always do the negotiating yourself. Know when to bring in recruits or to have someone do the negotiating for you. There are times when you need the assistance of a recognized expert or another team member to communicate important points. Sometimes you simply need the support, but if that is the case make sure you have a strong reason to include that person in the negotiations.

10. Don't put yourself at a disadvantage by pleading your case or by asking for another chance if negotiations come to a standstill with a definite no to your proposal. Be patient. Show your appreciation for the opportunity, take

some time to prove your position, and then after an extended period of time try to open another negotiations.

The worst negotiation no no is when you simply don't ever approach the other party to try negotiating for something better.   Refusing to negotiate the important things in life makes you settle for second best.   Don't you deserve better?

Chapter Three—When Negotiations Go South

There are a number of reasons why a negotiation turns ugly, but when it does it can go downhill pretty quickly if not properly managed. The best thing to do is take all the precautions necessary to create a positive encounter in the first place. Treat one another fairly and respectfully, and even if nothing becomes of the negotiation, you haven't burned your bridges. Most of the time, negotiations go bad when requests become demands and the demands are outrageous or unacceptable. For the most part, people expect to have a little banter back and forth during the negotiation process, so that's just normal procedure. However, there are some telltale signs that indicate when you need to take quick action to preserve your negotiating position. The following are five clear signs your negotiations may be in trouble and what remedies you have:

1. The negotiating party stops returning your emails or phone calls. This is rather common when a negotiation has gone awry. Your perception might be that your negotiation is just about

completed when suddenly all communications end, leaving you wondering what happened and where to go from here.

Remedy:

If you are getting no response, there may be little you can do except count your losses and move forward. However, if the opportunity is worth one more try, try communicating in a way that you haven't before. Try old-fashioned snail mail and give the other party time to consider starting fresh. When you mail your communications, do something that will make your contact memorable. One of my friends once found herself in this situation when negotiating a new job. She ended up sending an Edible with chocolate covered fruit and a note that said. "I'm so sorry this didn't work out, and if you would like to have a do-over, I'm game. Enjoy the Edibles. Nobody ever said I didn't have good taste."

As it turned out, the negotiation was going well but the supervisor had decided to promote within to a candidate who was underqualified and overconfident. They called my friend about 30 days later and offered her the job at the pay she had first requested.

The lesson to be learned here is to never jump to negative conclusions when negotiations go south. It could be something totally out of the control of the negotiating party.

2. <u>You show up for the negotiations and there are way too many people involved on the other side</u>. I was once negotiating a book deal that required me to travel from Arizona to Chicago. It was my understanding that I would be picked up at the airport, dropped at the hotel to freshen up, and then shuttled to their downtown office late that afternoon to meet with the company's CEO. As it turned out, nobody met me at the airport so I ended up taking a cab, which cost me a pretty penny. Then as soon as I got to the hotel, a driver picked me up to take me downtown for the negotiations. I was tired from the

flight, and my appearance was that of a person who had been traveling all day. When I arrived at the office, I was escorted into a conference room with five gentlemen all dressed in dark suits and freshly starched shirts. They sat opposite me on the other side of the table, with their matching portfolios and company pens, ready to take the appropriate notes.

I sat there for a few moments, and then I looked around and got this huge grin on my face. Gentlemen, before we proceed, I have to apologize for my appearance. I misunderstood the arrangements, and I'm afraid I have given you the impression that I didn't care enough about this meeting to dress appropriately. Nothing could be further from the truth. Having said that, I would like to make a small request of you. Could you please loosen your ties and take off your jackets, and you can even pull off your shoes if you like. This way I'll feel like we're on an even playing field.

What I did was accepted the situation as my mistake instead of blaming the others. I refused to let myself be intimidated by the men in black, and I used my sense of humor to get me through the next hour and a half of negotiations. At the same time, I showed them I would not be put at a disadvantage. I ended up with the contract and have done business with them throughout the years. The CEO admitted to me that they had set me up to see if I could handle stressful situations similar to those I would be facing if I were to accept their offer.

Remedy:

When the going gets tough, don't get angry and if you are you certainly can't show it. Use your sense of humor. If it has really gone bad, what do you have to lose?

3. <u>There's a major game change right in the middle of the negotiation</u>. If you're negotiating with your spouse or a friend or family member, you could feel as though you're moving forward and suddenly the stakes have risen or the subject has changed. You're no longer negotiating the initial

issue; you're arguing a past point of contention.

Remedy:

Get up and move, change positions, do whatever it takes to create a start over, to bring you back to the initial negotiation. If the argument continues and it becomes clear that you cannot move forward, leave it for another time. If possible, defuse the anger and respectfully ask to postpone the discussion, then go do something fun that takes the heat down a notch.

4. The other party is listening and agreeing with you, but the negotiation isn't going anywhere. This one is a tough one, because it's not emotionally charged, it's not that you

cannot agree, it's that there is nothing but agreement and yet still no action. The other person in the negotiations is benevolent, and you can't get him or her to pull the trigger and make a commitment.

Remedy:

Restate the terms you're requesting in the negotiation and clearly confirm the other party is in agreement. Put a date and time on when you will begin to receive what you are asking for, and refuse to accept a vague or indecisive response. If the party continues to stall or hesitate, list on your fingers the points you understood were agreeable between you, until you get to the one you think made the negotiation go south. Then, simply renegotiate that one point. Resist the temptation to try to negotiate the entire thing again, it will take too much energy and time and you'll lose the other party in this tedious process. Only renegotiate the point of contention if it can be identified.

5. <u>The other party in the negotiation asked you a question you are not prepared to answer</u>. This is only a temporary postponement of the negotiation, and if possible you can move forward and leave that one point on the backburner. Unless that one thing is a deal-breaker for you. For example, perhaps you were on a job interview and your employer just informed you that the job required travel, which was why you were

considering leaving your current position. Deal breaker—NEXT!

Remedy:

There are many remedies for this because there could be so many questions that you were not prepared to address at the time of the negotiation. The one point I wanted to make sure you understood here is that sometimes you simply have to say—NEXT!

Chapter Four—Different Types of Negotiators

Throughout my professional career, I believe I have experienced almost every type of negotiator—some pleasant and some—well, not so much. I've decided to give you some examples of these types of negotiators and let you know how my associates, friends, and I have dealt with them.

The Egotistical Negotiator

This is a person who thinks negotiations means you agree to do things his or her way, end of discussion. For these types of negotiators, it's a game they have to win or they simply aren't going to play. These types of negotiators require a bit of sucking up, ego stroking, letting them win a few of the points that you didn't care much about anyway. However, keep in mind, if you give it all away—nobody wins. The other party won't respect you, and, more importantly, you won't respect yourself.

The Take and Take Negotiator

With this type of negotiator, each time you give a little expecting them to give a little in return, they simply take a little more. So, you find yourself in a tug-a-war which goes something like this: you give, they take, you give more, they take more. If you plant yourself and refuse to give any more, the negotiations can get ugly. One of my clever co-workers did this. After giving a lot of little things, she visibly sat back in her chair and asked, "So, I've folded on this, and this, and this. Now, what can I expect from you?"

The Distracted Negotiator

You could be pouring your plan out to this person, and they're texting under their desk with a glance up now and then just to make sure you haven't left the room. Between the secretary's interruptions, the phone ringing, and their texting, you feel as though you're wasting your time. Newsflash—you are. I once scheduled a meeting with an attorney to discuss a business transaction in which I was about to participate. We had negotiated the attorney fees by letter, and I agreed to pay $200 per hour for his undivided attention. Problem was, I never got his undivided attention. When he invoiced me, I paid half and informed him that I only received approximately 30 minutes of his time. This was fine with me, but don't conduct other business during half our meeting and charge me for it. Obviously, I never returned and he never pushed the point. I think we both learned our lesson.

The Negative Negotiator

This type of negotiator mistakenly believes they'll get you for less if they make you feel they don't really want you. They make you feel as though agreeing to meet with you was just because they wanted to do you a favor. Don't be fooled. Know your worth, and stick to your guns. If you are well worth what you are asking, don't be put down in order to give the other party an advantage in the negotiations.

The Cheap Negotiator

This type of negotiator will complement you, make you feel valued and the perfect person for the job, and then apologize profusely for not being able to offer you what you're asking. On one hand they say they wouldn't blame you if you walked, while on the other hand they are expecting you to stay. With these types of negotiators, offering you more is always out of their hands. They don't have the last say, so it becomes impossible to negotiate because you don't have the final decision maker. You can ask them to invite the person in power to the negotiation, or you can set something up for another time. It's important to let them know that you are not prepared to take less because you don't want to feel like you were taken advantage of down the road and be forced to look for another job.

The Frustrated Negotiator

From the beginning of the negotiation, this type of negotiator is blustery and loudly complains about even the smallest request. There are lots of gestures with this type of negotiator: rolled eyes, lots of frowning, some will look through files or busy their hands by tapping a pen on the desk, anything that displays their growing annoyance and frustration. All these gestures are designed to distract and make you give in to a less than desirable outcome. Keep a straight, no nonsense expression and a calm demeanor. Just watch them go through their antics and then pick up where you left off.

The Ultimate Negotiator

This is a powerful negotiator who values the process and wants everyone to benefit from the negotiation. What do you do with a negotiator such as this one? Be thankful and return the favor.

Chapter Five—Past Failures

Future Successes

Failed negotiations don't necessarily have to dictate our chances for future negotiation successes. Of course, if you continue to make the same mistakes when negotiating, there's nothing that can keep you from experiencing the same kinds of outcomes. The best thing you can do to turn your failures into successes is to educate yourself, which is what you are doing now, right? Make a commitment to become an effective negotiator, to practice negotiating all different situations, and then analyze what was done correctly and what needs improving.

If you believe negotiating is about to become a much bigger part of your game plan, you may want to keep a negotiations notebook. I did this, and every time I heard somebody talk about turning around a difficult negotiation, I recorded it in my notebook for reference. When I thought there would be a stumbling block during a negotiation, I referred to my notebook before I left to get ideas that might help me hurdle the challenges and move toward success.

I decided to include some of these scenarios in this book as a kick-start for your own personal notebook. Here are some negotiations my associates and I have experienced in both our personal and professional negotiations. Some were huge mistakes and some were huge successes, but all were learning experiences.

Contract Negotiations

I once negotiated the sale of a business where my buyer requested I sign a restrictive clause that limited my ability to work within five miles of the business in the same or related field. I was so eager to sell the business that I agreed to those terms. Keep in mind, I carried the full financing for the business, and I required nothing down. Essentially, I gave her the business with no personal investment on her part. Even though I didn't want a restrictive clause in the contract I agreed, until one last request put me over the edge. If, for any reason, the restrictive clause was breached, she requested that I agree to consider the entire debt paid in full and all the inventory and equipment belonged to her. I refused, and she purchased the business anyway.

Although I was eager to sell the business and she agreed to pay me my full asking price, it was a fair price and she could not have purchased it without my amazing terms. I probably could have ask more for the business because I was willing to finance it, but I certainly wasn't going to risk limiting my ability to make a living. It was an example of too much push and too little push power.

Job Negotiations

Early in my husband's career, he was offered a job with an airline in the Midwest that required us to move from Arizona to Cincinnati. The negotiations went well, but the only drawback was the company refused to pay for our move. They needed to fill the position right away, so we sold everything and moved 2,000 miles across country within two weeks. We accepted less for our home, sold all our belongings at pennies on the dollar, and packed our clothes and dogs and off we went. When we got there, we found a new place, bought a house full of furniture, and settled ourselves and the dogs in a matter of days.

There was no time to even take a breath before my husband was to report to work. When he got there, he was called into his supervisor's office for a little talk. Next thing he knew, he was right in the middle of renegotiating his employment contract. They wanted him to accept less bonus and pay. Keep in mind, we had already sold everything and moved 2,000 miles. Needless to say, he was at a definite disadvantage. Instead of throwing up his hands, he simply said he appreciated their position but he was unable to accept their offer under those terms. Then he asked a very important question. "How can we make this work to both our benefits?"

They put their heads together and discovered he had some experience in several different areas of crew scheduling as well as crew planning. He had originally been asked to manage crew planning, but he was also willing to design some spreadsheets and reports that would help make crew scheduling run more efficiently. He stepped up and so did they, creating a successful negotiation.

Services Negotiations

I once negotiated a book contract with a small company that was working with maximum needs and limited funds. Their writing needs were extensive, so I knew there would be much work there for me in the future if I was able to negotiate a fair resolution to their rather underfunded current writing needs. Because I wasn't quite sure what the future held, I offered to write the first project at full price, but I would also give them added value by including a creative idea I had for another project. Each time they sent new clients my way I gave them a small discount on their next project. I built quite a writing business from that one client, and he earned a substantial discount on almost all of his writing projects as a result of the success of our initial negotiations.

Being creative in negotiations may mean taking a calculated risk. You're always wondering if you are giving too much away, leaving too much on the table. But, guess what, I guarantee you the other party in the negotiations is wondering the same thing. Could I have gotten them to agree to do the job for less? Should I have held on a little bit longer?

The answers to these types of questions can remain a mystery until you jump in and do business together. But you'll never know the answers if you don't take that chance and make some concessions that could bring incredible returns. When involved in important negotiations that involve a good deal of money, I always ask myself how much more money I will make or how much more satisfaction I will experienced by getting what I'm asking for in this negotiation? Most of the time, my assumptions are correct, and even if I have a blooper once in a while, the positive results far outweigh the negative.

Purchase Negotiations

I considered this example to be one of a rather back-handed negotiations. My sister purchased a purebred toy poodle from a local breeder. She paid a good deal of money for the dog, but he was adorable and the breeder seemed reputable. The standard acceptable weight of a toy poodle is supposed to be approximately 6 to 10 pounds and be less than 11 inches tall. After about five months it was clear my sister's dog was far from being a toy, and, in fact, as an adult he would probably be sized more along the miniature poodle scale.

Although my sister loved her dog, she had paid the price for a toy and she definitely didn't get what she paid for. She returned to the breeder with her complaint, and his answer was that she could return her dog and he would refund her money. This was a very sneaky negotiations, knowing that her emotions were involved and she wasn't about to return the dog. Upon reporting her experience to the breeders' association, and giving the breeder a bad review online, she discovered she was not his only disgruntled customer.

The problem was, my sister had failed to do her homework beforehand. When she purchased the dog at such a good price, she never questioned the validity of the dog's credentials. Instead she chose to believe she was simply an amazing negotiator. Know what you want and what it's worth. When something seems too good to be true, it usually is just that—not true.

Unfortunately, in today's society, you must always watch your back in an important negotiation. Nobody cares more about the negotiation than you, and if you don't pay attention you are opening the door for someone to take advantage of you. Be vigilant, be truthful and fair, and try to negotiate with others who do the same.

Chapter Six—Profile of a Strong Negotiator

Strong negotiators can be proficient in many things, but the following is a profile of a strong negotiator.

Characteristics	Skills	Reputation
Calm	Communicator	Fair
Patient	Organized	Open-Minded
Understanding	Goal Oriented	Good Judgement
Knowledgeable	Persuasive	Assertive
Integrity	Determined	Insightful
Flexible	Decisive	Intelligent
Articulate	Compromising	Good Listener
Positive	Problem Solver	Creative

Just because you haven't been a strong negotiator in the past doesn't mean you won't be in the future. There are so many different types and situations where negotiations are required, that you can begin again with each new negotiation. Stop pouting over a failed negotiation, pick yourself up, and jump back on the bandwagon. The best way to overcome your negotiation shyness and fear is to keep on negotiating, to try and try again.

Being creative and imaginative can make all the difference in becoming a strong negotiator. When you learn to listen between the lines of what the other's payoff is, you can begin to form a plan that will give that person most of what they want while still allowing you to get what you want. It takes being determined to find a way where everybody wins— where everybody comes away from the table pleased with the outcome and proud of their ability to continue to negotiate.

Learning to be a strong negotiator is definitely more difficult in today's society. We certainly are not seeing fair and strong negotiations modeled by our government officials. For years Congress has been at a standstill, accomplishing little except to frustrate and upset the

American people. Why? They do not know how to fairly negotiate. Most of the time they know what they want but don't know how to figure out what the other guy wants in the negotiations.

Once they discover what they want and what the other party to the negotiations wants, both sides are unwilling to make the exchange. We have become a two-party system where both sides refuse to compromise. Our President wants every single thing done his way. Our Congress won't take one step forward to compromise by meeting him in the middle. They have not been taught, nor are they teaching strong leadership skills through successful negotiations.

Further down the totem pole, our corporations, professional institutions, families, and friends are not practicing fair and just negotiations either. One side wants this, the other wants that but won't give this, they yell and argue and go to their respective corners to prepare for a long drawn-out battle of the wills. Meanwhile, the negotiations break down into an endless boxing match with an arena full of fans who are bored with the bickering and soon leave the facility. Witnessing a fair fight is no longer an option; instead, we are fighting an unfair witness that opposes another' rights to achieve negotiating success. Not because we refuse to negotiate, but because we don't know how to negotiate in a just and rewarding manner.

So how in the world can we learn to become strong negotiators? The younger you are, the easier it is to learn. The minds of children are like little sponges, soaking up all the information and knowledge that surround them on a daily basis. Instead of teaching them not to ask for things, why not teach your children the right way to ask and get what they want. Instead of punishing them in their first attempts at negotiations, just think how much stronger they could become if they were rewarded for their practice and successes.

I once heard good parents don't raise children, they are raising adults. How true! You don't want to be childlike all your life, right? If you want to hunt with the big dogs, you can't be afraid of every small critter and moving bush in your path. Instead of letting them stop you in your tracks, you've got to learn to negotiate around them by overcoming your fears and shyness. Becoming a strong negotiator is done one baby step at a time, one small success after another until your confidence grows and so do your negotiation skills.

Chapter Seven—Putting Power into Your Negotiations

One of the ways you can put power into your negotiations is to be charming and likeable. Everyone would prefer to do business with people they like—so give them what they want and be likeable. There are so many choices we have when it comes to finding suppliers for our wants and needs. Consider it an honor that the other party has chosen you and your company or family or friend to participate in the negotiations. Being chosen to negotiate with another should be considered a privilege. After all, they bypassed all the others who were qualified to do business with them or to be their friend, and instead they came to you. Those who believe it's an honor to negotiate with you will treat your requests with respect and integrity.

I'm sure you've heard you can't see the forest for the trees. That's the problem people have when attempting to create a successful and powerful negotiations. They can't see the bigger picture. Instead of recognizing the future impact of today's decision, they tend to simply see the outcome and its present influence on their business or personal lives. If you want to put power into your negotiations, know what is being negotiated and then expand those wants and needs to determine their effect on the future.

Don't be shy about asking a lot of questions to determine what will be best for all parties in the negotiations. Remember, your power comes from making sure everybody walks away from the negotiations feeling good about the outcome. You can't possible know what the other party truly wants if you don't ask—so ask away. Asking questions shows you are interested, that you are willing to hear their side of the story, which brings us to another important

Deborah Siegel

component of putting the power back into your negotiations.

Make up your mind to do more than hear—LISTEN. Stop planning what you'll say next to counter the last point made, and actually commit yourself to listening to what the other person is saying. Many more discoveries are made when you look and listen for every opportunity to negotiate fairly and thoroughly. It doesn't really matter how many questions you ask if you're not listening to the answers, now does it?

Once you've asked questions and practiced interactive listening, you can identify the existing problem. You see, every want and need begins first with a problem. Even when the problem is a good one to have, you still need a solution to the problem. If you're in the market for a new home, it's because your old one is no longer meeting your needs. The need to negotiate for another home was initiated by a problem. If you child is looking for the best university to attend and is trying to negotiate with you about helping to pay for the education needed, that began with a need that was first a problem. The problem isn't really the money, but rather negotiating the appropriate university to fit the needs of your child.

Once you have identified the problem, to be a powerful negotiator, you must be or find the solution to the problem. If you cannot get the other party to agree that you are their solution, they can simply find another party and continue the negotiations elsewhere. In short, to put power into your negotiations, you need to be an insightful, likeable, and assertive problem solver. That can be a lot to ask in any negotiation, but practice creates potential.

Chapter Eight—Dealing with the Fear Factor

We fear what we don't understand and are not sure of the outcome. These are huge elements of negotiations. No matter how much you research and prepare, there are always going to be questions that throw you and that send your negotiations in a different direction. As the unknown rises, so will your fear. You are being forced out of your comfort zone, and that can be a scary place. Confidence can be scarce when operating outside the familiar things that bring you comfort and clarity.

Another way to deal with the fear factor is to understand where it comes from. As children, most of us were told repeatedly to sit down and be quiet. We annoyed our parents by asking too many questions. We wanted what we wanted, so we tried to wheel and deal with our parents, and most of the time we were not rewarded for our behaviors. That should explain away what causes fear in us as we negotiate.

When you engage another in a negotiation, it's common to wonder what they will think of you. Will they see you as demanding and greedy for asking for what you want? Most people admire you for having the courage to negotiate. The more difficult the negotiations the more tempting it is to hide in your shell and pretend like you never wanted to negotiate to begin with.

When it comes to money, whether you are asking for a raise or for a discount, the fear you feel is almost the same. Another thing we are taught as children, don't ask for things. Suddenly we grow up and we are praised and admired for asking. How confusing can that be? It is a proven fact that people who asked for and negotiated a raise received an average of $5,000 or more in increased wages.

Let's face it, it's a whole lot more fun to go to the zoo or play a round of golf than it is for most people to negotiate. Sure, there is satisfaction when you get what you want, but the actual act of negotiating can be grueling and extremely uncomfortable. We experience one negative negotiation, and that same fear follows us for years. You know exactly what I mean if you've ever been confronted during a negotiation.

I was publisher for a national trade magazine years ago, and it was my job to negotiate advertising contracts with local businesses. I had been trying to get an appointment with a CEO of this prominent business, and was finally successful. I walked into his office, sat down, and thought I was showing my interest in his business when I asked my first question: "Now, how many employees do you have, Mr. Bryant?" With that, he promptly stood up, dismissed me, and walked to the door. As I reached the door he said, "You should have known the answer to that question. Stop wasting my time. Come back when you've done your homework."

I was bound and determined to get him to advertise, so I returned a few weeks later. I saw the look of surprise on his face at seeing me again, but I was better prepared to negotiate his business this time around. Instead of wasting his time with foolish, meaningless questions, I started out by saying, "I would love to get your authorization on this advertising agreement, but most of all I wanted to come back and say thanks for teaching me a very important lesson."

I confronted Mr. Bryant and my own fears, returning to negotiate what I wanted and what I knew would benefit him as well. Mr. Bryant became one of my little ambassadors, spreading the word to other local business leaders what a great new way we had to advertise their products and services. Of course, he was still a tough negotiator, and I ended up offering him a tidy sum off his full-page ad, but we both profited from the negotiation.

Conclusion—Setting Yourself Up for Success

To effectively negotiate every situation, it takes preparation and a goal-oriented mindset. If you don't know where you're going, how will you know when you've arrived? Successful negotiations require ongoing examination and analysis about what has worked in the past and what can be implemented in future negotiations. Look at your negotiations history; have you been setting yourself up for success or failure? Do you create opportunities or just more problems in your negotiations? Did the outcome of your last negotiation open doors for you, or did you walk away feeling short changed? Along with those listed below, these are the questions you should be asking yourself to discover the

93

improvements needed to give you greater future successes in your negotiations.

- What is your objective?
- How will you prepare your case?
- What do you want?
- What are you willing to give to get what you want?
- What is your bottom line?
- What are the other party's strengths and weaknesses?
- What does the other person want from the negotiation?
- What are they willing to give up to get what they want?
- Will you negotiate from a point of knowledge and insight?
- Do you have commonalities with the other party in the negotiation?
- What is your worth?

- Have you selected the proper location for your negotiation, with few distractions?
- Have you prepared and practiced to address every scenario?
- How will you measure your progress during the negotiation?
- What can you do to show you are flexible and willing to compromise?
- Have you identified or considered the other party's negotiating style, character, skills, and reputation?
- Have you put yourself in the other's place?
- Do you have well-defined and specific goals?
- Have your demands been presented respectfully and are they reasonable?
- What will be your approach and opening statement?

- Does your opening statement encourage the other party to embrace your ideas?
- Are you being too competitive?
- Have you set up the negotiations for successful outcomes, or do you consider the negotiations as a win/lose proposition?

Bottom line is there is no way you can go through life avoiding negotiations. Obviously, we have focused more on professional negotiations, but there are many if not more required in your personal life. Avoiding negotiations doesn't make them go away; it just makes you weaker in your attempt at success.

The way to set yourself up for successful negotiations is to be confident in your abilities and plan like there's no tomorrow. I promise, all the research and planning you do ahead of time will bring huge payoffs in the end. Besides, the more you plan, the more defined and definite you can be when explaining your wants and needs and identifying the problems and challenges you must overcome in order to achieve success.

Make your self-talk positive and creative. That voice inside your head should encourage you during your negotiations, enabling you to gain the confidence needed when it's time to press forward or hold back. Trust yourself in every negotiation. Listen and observe the other person to determine how you can maneuver the process in order to avoid any stumbling blocks and potential pitfalls.

Negotiations are happening around you every day; make it a habit to listen to how people resolve their issues and negotiate for better results next time. Incorporate what has worked for you in the past for what you want to happen in the future. Then go out there and negotiate. Negotiate for better relationships, better jobs, better pay, better service, and better purchases.

'